THE DOMINIE WORLD OF INVERTEBRATES

SPIDERS & SCORPIONS

Written by Graham Meadows & Claire Vial

CONTENTS

Dominie Press, Inc.

SPIDERS AND SCORPIONS

Spiders and scorpions belong to a group of invertebrates called arachnids. This group also includes false scorpions, harvestmen, mites, and ticks. Arachnids have existed for more than 350 million years.

▲ Scorpion

Most spiders and scorpions are **venomous**. They have glands that produce poison. All spiders and scorpions are **carnivores**. They catch and eat live animals. Most of them live on land and are **solitary**.

A hard outer skeleton, called an exoskeleton, protects their bodies. The exoskeleton also helps to keep them from drying out.

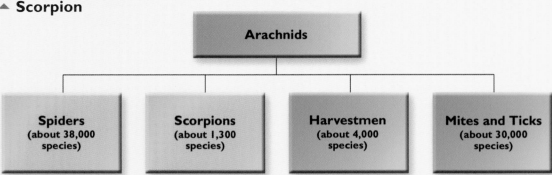

Arachnids

| Spiders (about 38,000 species) | Scorpions (about 1,300 species) | Harvestmen (about 4,000 species) | Mites and Ticks (about 30,000 species) |

▲ **Golden Orb Spider on Web**

ABOUT SPIDERS

Spiders come in many shapes and colors, and they vary greatly in size. Some are as small as the head of a pin. Others are much larger. The goliath, or bird-eating tarantula, can measure up to ten inches across. The goliath is the largest spider on Earth.

Cobalt Blue Tarantula ▼

Most spiders have: six to eight eyes, two parts to their body, spinnerets at the tip of the abdomen, four pairs of walking legs, and jaws with fangs.

Goliath, or Bird-eating Tarantula ▲

WHERE SPIDERS LIVE

Spiders are found on every continent except Antarctica. They are more common in **tropical** and subtropical areas than in **temperate** areas.

▲ **Red-kneed Tarantula**

◀ **Water Spider**

6

PRIMITIVE AND MODERN SPIDERS

There are two main types of spiders: primitive spiders and modern spiders.

Primitive spiders, such as tarantulas, are large, have long lives, and move their jaws up and down.

Modern spiders, such as the huntsman spider, are smaller, have shorter lives, and move their jaws from side to side. Most living **species** of spiders are modern spiders.

Most spiders live on land. Some, called water spiders, live in calm fresh water.

Huntsman Spider ▶

HOW SPIDERS CATCH THEIR PREY

Some spiders, such as the orb web spider, build webs to trap their **prey**.

Some spiders hunt for their prey. They stalk their prey until they are close enough to catch it.

Some spiders, such as the trapdoor spider, sit and wait for their prey. When their prey comes close to them, they pounce on it.

Once they have caught their prey, most spiders inject venom through their fangs. The venom either kills or **paralyzes** their prey. Some large spiders, such as the sun spider, do not inject venom. They use their strong jaws to rip their prey apart.

Sun Spider Eating a Cricket ▶

The fangs of most spiders cannot pierce human skin.

▲ **Trapdoor Spider**

◀ **Orb Web Spider with Prey**

WHAT SPIDERS EAT

Insects make up the main part of the spider's **diet**. Some larger species of spiders also feed on lizards and birds.

Like other spiders, the funnel-web spider uses a special digestive fluid to turn the soft body parts of its prey into a liquid. Then it sucks up the liquid.

Spiders do not eat the hard parts of their prey.

Funnel-web Spider ▼

Wolf Spider ▲

HOW THEY PROTECT THEMSELVES

Most spiders are **nocturnal**. They hide during the day. Some spiders, including wolf spiders, build **burrows** to hide in; others, such as the leaf-curling spider, hide in leaves.

Other spiders, such as the orb web spider, are **camouflaged** so that they blend in with their surroundings.

When some types of tarantulas are threatened by **predators**, they scrape off hairs from their abdomen. These hairs have tiny barbs that can cause skin irritations and help protect the tarantulas.

Spider Web Covered in Dew ▲

SPIDER SILK

Spiders have special glands inside their bodies that can produce different types of silk. They have spinnerets on their abdomen that spin the silk. Spiders use the silk to make webs, build shelters, protect their eggs, and create draglines to catch themselves if they fall.

▲ **Orb Web Spider**

Different species of spiders spin different types of webs. Common types of webs include orb webs, cobwebs, ladder webs, sheet webs, tunnel webs, and line webs.

All spiders spin silk, but not all spiders make webs. Spider silk is the strongest natural fiber known.

THE LIFE CYCLE OF A SPIDER

The larger the female spider, the more eggs she lays. The number of eggs can range from a few to more than two thousand. Most female spiders wrap their eggs in a special egg sac made of silk. Some spiders hang the egg sac in a web. Others attach the sac to a plant. Still others carry the egg sac around with them.

In some spider species, such as the redback spider and the nursery web spider, the female guards the eggs until the next stage of the **life cycle** begins and the babies, or spiderlings, hatch out. As they grow, the young spiders shed their skin several times. This shedding process is called molting.

Female and Male Two-spined Spiders ▼

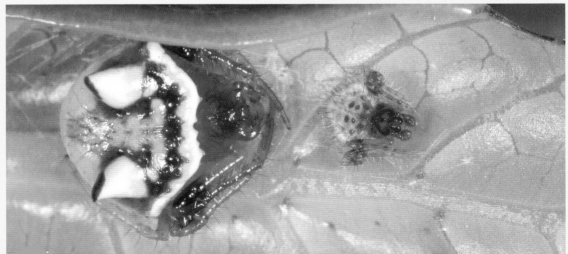

▲ **Redback Spider**

◄ **Nursery Web Spider**

15

ABOUT SCORPIONS

Scorpions use their **pincers** and sharp stinger to protect themselves against predators.

Most species of scorpions are similar in shape. Males are usually more slender and have longer tails than females.

All scorpions have:

- A segmented tail that is usually curved up and over the body, with a poisonous stinger on the end

- A flat, segmented body

- Two large claws, or pincers

- Eight legs

Scorpion ▲

WHERE SCORPIONS LIVE

Scorpions are most common in the warmer areas of North America, Central America, South America, Europe, Africa, and Australia.

Scorpion Eating a Cricket ▲

WHAT SCORPIONS EAT

Scorpions wait for their prey to come to them, rather than hunt for their food. They catch and eat small animals, such as insects, spiders, and centipedes. They use a special fluid to break down the soft parts of their prey into a liquid. They then suck up the liquid, leaving behind much of the exoskeleton.

Their method of hunting depends on the size of the prey. Small prey is simply caught and held in the pincers. Large or struggling prey is held and also stung.

Occasionally, scorpions eat each other, particularly when they are shedding their skin. Scorpions are also prey for other animals, such as birds and monkeys.

Some scorpions can go for several months, or even an entire year, without food!

THE LIFE CYCLE OF A SCORPION

When male and female scorpions meet, the male holds the female by her pincers. They perform a special "dance" before they **mate**.

Unlike spiders, the female scorpion does not lay her eggs. She holds them inside her body for several months and then gives birth to live young. Most females give birth to between twenty-five and one hundred young scorpions.

Newborn scorpions are white in color. They climb up onto their mother's back, where they remain for one to fifty days.

As they grow, the young scorpions shed their skin several times. This shedding process is called molting.

Female Scorpion Carrying Young ▲

▲ **Male and Female Scorpions Doing a "Courtship Dance"**

SPIDERS AND SCORPIONS, AND THEIR IMPORTANCE TO HUMANS

How They Are Useful

- Spiders and scorpions play an important part in the **food chain**.

- They feed on many insects, and they are food for other animals, such as birds and meerkats.

Meerkat Eating a Scorpion ▼

How They Are Harmful

- A few types of spiders are dangerous to humans because their bite can cause sickness, or even death. These include the black widow spider and the brown recluse spider of North America, and the funnel-web spider of Australia. Scientists have produced anti-venom for some dangerous species of spiders, such as the funnel-web spider.

- A few species of scorpions are deadly to humans. Most scorpions have a painful sting that is not fatal to humans.

**Scientist Extracting Venom ▶
from a Funnel-web Spider**

GLOSSARY

burrows: Tunnels or holes in the ground where wild animals live
camouflaged: Disguised by natural features that blend in with the surroundings
carnivores: Animals that eat other animals
diet: The food that an animal or a person usually eats
food chain: A term used to describe how all living things, predators and prey, feed on other living things in order to survive
life cycle: The stages, or phases, of an animal's development
mate: To join with another animal in order to produce offspring
nocturnal: Active at night
paralyze: To make an animal unable to move
pincers: Claws used for holding on to things
predators: Animals that hunt, catch, and eat other animals
prey: Animals that are hunted and eaten by other animals
solitary: Living alone; without company
species: Types of animals that have some physical characteristics in common
temperate: Land areas or bodies of water with a mild temperature and moderate climate
tropical: Areas that are very warm throughout the year
venomous: Poisonous; deadly

INDEX